A TREASURY OF XXth CENTURY MURDER

Madison Square Tragedy

ISBN: 978-1-56163-762-1
Library of Congress Control Number: 2013947335
© 2013 Rick Geary
Printed in China

1st printing December 2013

Comicslit is an imprint
and trademark of

NANTIER · BEALL · MINOUSTCHINE
Publishing inc.
new york

MADISON SQUARE TRAGEDY

The Murder of STANFORD WHITE

25 June 1906

WRITTEN AND ILLUSTRATED BY
RICK GEARY

HENRY
KENDALL
THAW
FEBRUARY 12 - 1871
FEBRUARY 22 - 1947
AND NOW ABIDETH FAITH, HOPE
CHARITY, THESE THREE, BUT THE
GREATEST OF THESE IS CHARITY.

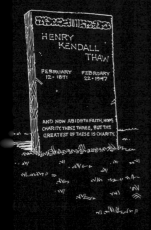

MADISON SQUARE TRAGEDY
BIBLIOGRAPHY

Crimes of Passion, no author credited. (London, Verdict Press, 1975)

Langford, Gerald, *The Murder of Stanford White.* (New York, Indianapolis, The Bobbs-Merrill Co., Inc., 1962)

Lowe, David Garrard, *Stanford White's New York.* (New York, Watson-Guptill Publications, 1999)

Mooney, Michael Macdonald, *Evelyn Nesbit and Stanford White: Love and Death in the Gilded Age.* (New York, William Morrow and Co., Inc, 1976)

Thaw, Harry K. *The Traitor.* (Philadelphia, Dorrance & Company, 1926)

Uruburu, Paula, *American Eve: Evelyn Nesbit, Stanford White, the Birth of the "It" Girl, and the Crime of the Century.* (New York, Riverhead Books, 2008)

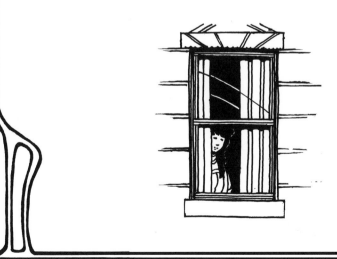

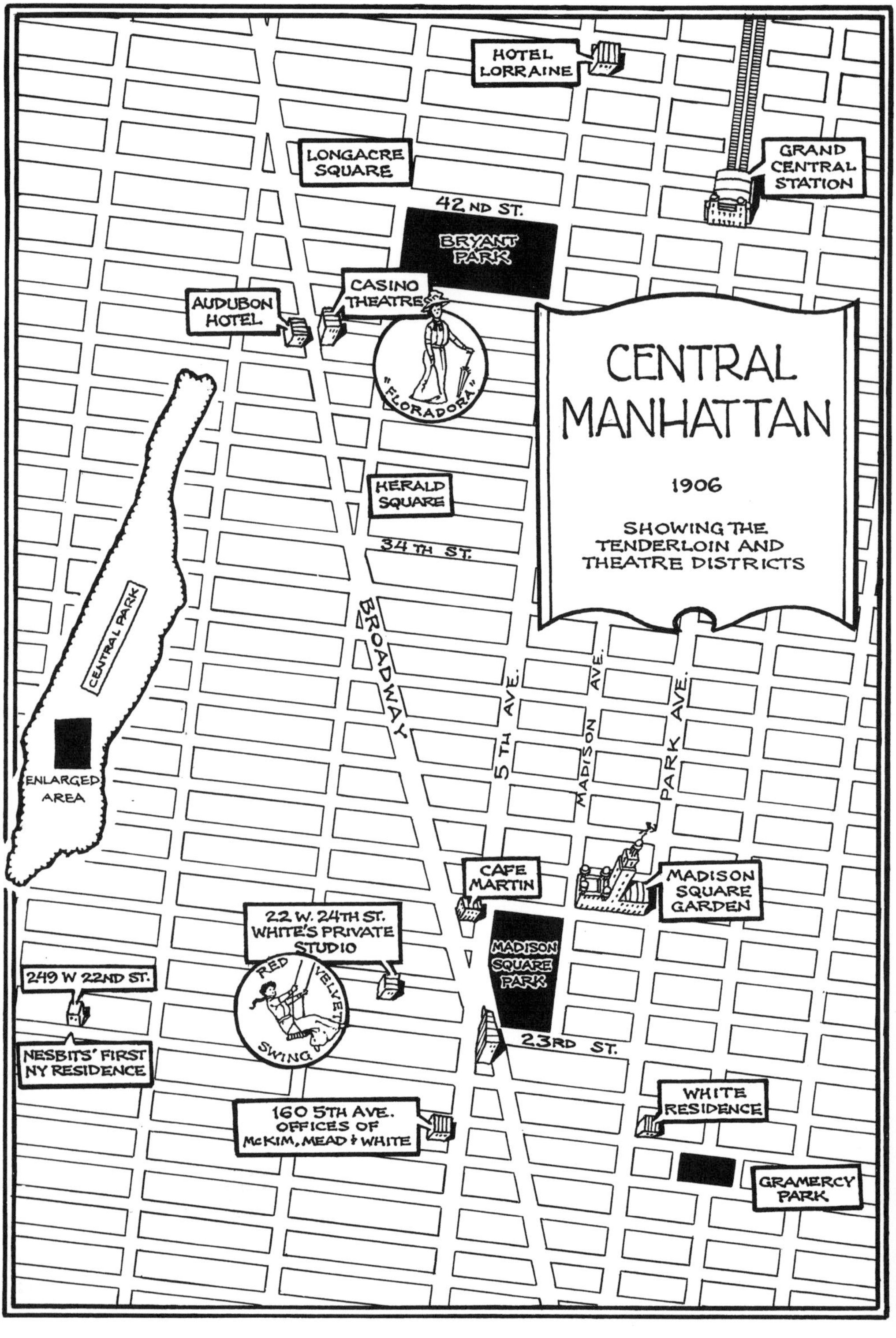
CENTRAL MANHATTAN
1906
SHOWING THE TENDERLOIN AND THEATRE DISTRICTS
HOTEL LORRAINE
GRAND CENTRAL STATION
LONGACRE SQUARE
42 ND ST.
BRYANT PARK
CASINO THEATRE
AUDUBON HOTEL
"FLORADORA"
HERALD SQUARE
34 TH ST.
BROADWAY
5 TH AVE.
MADISON AVE.
PARK AVE.
CENTRAL PARK
ENLARGED AREA
CAFE MARTIN
MADISON SQUARE GARDEN
MADISON SQUARE PARK
22 W. 24TH ST. WHITE'S PRIVATE STUDIO
RED VELVET SWING
249 W 22ND ST.
NESBITS' FIRST NY RESIDENCE
23RD ST.
WHITE RESIDENCE
160 5TH AVE. OFFICES OF McKIM, MEAD & WHITE
GRAMERCY PARK

PART I

THE CITY OF
THE NEW CENTURY

THE YEAR 1901.

AS THE GREAT ENGINE OF THE TWENTIETH CENTURY
ROARS TO LIFE, THE CITY OF NEW YORK PROVIDES
ITS PROPULSION.

BURSTING WITH OPTIMISM AND ENTERPRISE, THE CITY LOOKS TO THE FUTURE.

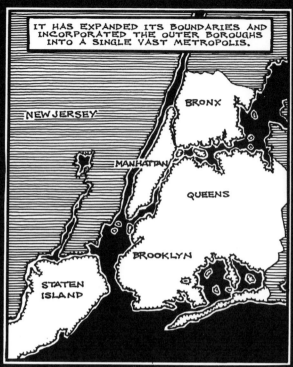

IT HAS EXPANDED ITS BOUNDARIES AND INCORPORATED THE OUTER BOROUGHS INTO A SINGLE VAST METROPOLIS.

NEW JERSEY

BRONX

MANHATTAN

QUEENS

BROOKLYN

STATEN ISLAND

WAVES OF IMMIGRANTS HAVE INCREASED THE POPULATION TO FOUR MILLION SOULS.

A NEW ERA OF SOCIAL MOBILITY... ARTISTIC INNOVATION... ENGINEERING MARVELS.

SKY-SCRAPERS STRETCH TO THE HEAVENS.

SPEED AND MOTION ARE THE ORDER OF THE DAY.

A SYSTEM OF UNDERGROUND TRAINS, NOW UNDER CONSTRUCTION, WILL LINK ALL CORNERS OF THE CITY.

THE AUTOMOBILE, UNTIL RECENTLY A PLAYTHING FOR THE WEALTHY, IS NOW SEEN WITH INCREASING FREQUENCY ALONG THE AVENUES.

FLYING MACHINES FILL THE SKY.

AND THE MOVING PICTURE CAMERA RECORDS IT ALL.

PRESIDENT THEODORE ROOSEVELT, THE FIRST CHIEF EXECUTIVE BORN IN THE CITY, TYPIFIES THE SPIRIT OF THE AGE.

THE NEW CULTURE OF CITY LIFE BRINGS HERETOFORE UNKNOWN PLEASURES AND DANGERS.

THE STORIES OF O. HENRY TELL OF ORDINARY PEOPLE MEETING THE COMPLICATED CHALLENGES OF THE URBAN ENVIRONMENT.

THE TRANSFORMATION OF SOCIETY IS GIVEN CHARACTER AND STYLE BY THE ILLUSTRATOR CHARLES DANA GIBSON.

THE "GIBSON GIRL" EXEMPLIFIES A NEW FREEDOM FOR WOMEN.

THE PRESIDENT'S FORTHRIGHT DAUGHTER, ALICE, SCANDALIZES THE NATION BY SMOKING IN PUBLIC.

IN NEW YORK, THE THEATRE EXPERIENCES AN IMMENSE BURST OF POPULARITY.

MUSICAL SHOWS DRAW GREAT CROWDS NIGHTLY.

THE THEATRE DISTRICT EXTENDS UP BROADWAY, FROM MADISON SQUARE AT 23RD STREET TO 42ND STREET AND LONGACRE SQUARE...

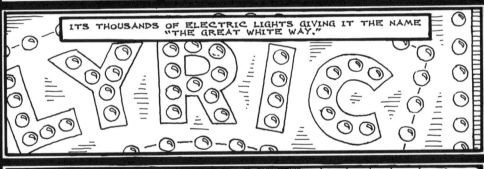

ITS THOUSANDS OF ELECTRIC LIGHTS GIVING IT THE NAME "THE GREAT WHITE WAY."

SURROUNDING IT IS THE BUSTLING AREA CALLED THE "TENDERLOIN," THE CENTER FOR PLEASURE AND VICE TO EVERY TASTE.

MERE BLOCKS AWAY IS FIFTH AVENUE, THE HOME OF UPSCALE MERCHANTS LIKE TIFFANY AND COMPANY...

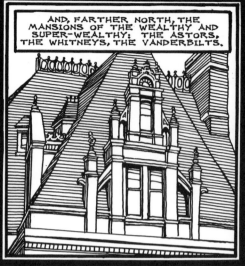

AND, FARTHER NORTH, THE MANSIONS OF THE WEALTHY AND SUPER-WEALTHY: THE ASTORS, THE WHITNEYS, THE VANDERBILTS.

THE CITY'S LEADING ARCHITECTURAL FIRM IS McKIM, MEAD AND WHITE, WHO OPERATE FROM THEIR OFFICE AT 160 FIFTH AVE.

THEY ARE CHIEF AMONG MANY TO HAVE TRANSFORMED THE CITY OVER THE PAST TWO DECADES...

FROM A SEA OF DULL BROWNSTONE TO GLEAMING AVENUES OF MARBLE AND TERRA-COTTA THAT REFLECT THE GLORIES OF A EUROPEAN GOLDEN AGE.

THE MOST VISIBLE OF THE FIRM'S PARTNERS IS STANFORD WHITE.

AN AVID THEATREGOER, CLUBMAN, PATRON OF THE FINEST RESTAURANTS.

HIS SIX-FOOT FRAME, BRIGHT RED HAIR, AND BRISTLING MOUSTACHE MAKE HIM A STANDOUT IN ANY CROWD.

ON TUESDAY MORNING, JUNE 26, 1906, THE CITY IS STUNNED BY THE NEWS THAT WHITE HAS BEEN MURDERED.

York American

RD WHITE ON ROOF GARDEN!

SHOOTS ARCHITECT IN BACK AS HE SITS TALKING TO WOMAN

TRAGIC OPENING NIGHT

NEWSPAPERS BLARE THE SHOCKING HEADLINES.

THE TRAGEDY OCCURRED THE NIGHT BEFORE, AT THE ROOFTOP THEATRE OF THE ARCHITECT'S BEST-KNOWN STRUCTURE: MADISON SQUARE GARDEN ON 26TH STREET.

THE CITY IS ENTRANCED AS THE STORY UNFOLDS.

THERE IS NO MYSTERY AS TO THE PERPETRATOR, WHO SURRENDERED AT THE SCENE: THE "MAD" MILLIONAIRE HARRY K. THAW OF PITTSBURGH.

HE DID IT, HE CLAIMS, TO AVENGE THE HONOR OF HIS WIFE, THE FORMER MODEL AND SHOW-GIRL EVELYN NESBIT.

IN THE DAYS TO COME, THAW LIVES A PRIVILEDGED EXISTENCE AT THE CITY JAIL...

AS HIS WIFE'S EVERY MOVEMENT IS MOBBED BY THE CURIOUS PRESS AND PUBLIC...

AND THE SCANDALOUS PRIVATE LIFE IF STANFORD WHITE IS REVEALED FOR ALL TO SEE.

TELL OF FORD WHITE'S DE...

"HUNTER" O SECRET

BUT LET US REVIEW THE LIVES OF THESE THREE AND TRACE THE PATHS THAT LED THEM TO THE FATAL NIGHT.

PART II

"STANNY"

AT THE DAWN OF THE NEW CENTURY, STANFORD WHITE, AT
AGE 47, HAD REACHED THE PINNACLE OF HIS FAME AND
INFLUENCE.

HE WAS BORN ON NOVEMBER 9, 1853, IN NEW YORK CITY...

THE YOUNGER OF TWO SONS BORN TO RICHARD GRANT WHITE AND ALEXINA MEASE WHITE.

THE FAMILY HOME ON EAST 10TH STREET.

THE FATHER WAS A NOTED ESSAYIST, NOVELIST, EDITOR, MUSIC AND DRAMA CRITIC -- BUT THE FAMILY WAS NOT WEALTHY.

HE FOUND STEADIER WORK AT THE NEW YORK CUSTOM HOUSE.

LITTLE "STANNY" WAS FULL OF ENERGY, EVER IN MOTION.

HE GREW UP IN A MILIEU OF GENTEEL BOHEMIANISM, AMID THE SOCIETY OF ARTISTS, WRITERS AND INTELLECTUALS.

FROM CHILDHOOD, HE SHOWED A TALENT FOR DRAWING, AND, BY AGE 17, HIS AMBITION WAS TO BE A PAINTER.

HIS PARENTS, HOWEVER, COULD NOT AFFORD COLLEGE OR ART SCHOOL.

INSTEAD, THROUGH HIS FATHER'S CONNECTIONS, HE ENTERED AN APPRENTICESHIP IN THE IN THE OFFICE OF AMERICA'S PRE-EMINENT ARCHITECT, HENRY H. RICHARDSON.

FROM HIS HEADQUARTERS ON HANOVER STREET IN LOWER MANHATTAN RICHARDSON HAD TRANSFORMED AMERICA WITH HIS PECULIARLY PERSONAL ROMANESQUE STYLE.

HE BECAME A MENTOR TO WHITE, WHO WORKED FOR HIM ON BOSTON'S TRINITY CHURCH...

AND THE NEW YORK STATE CAPITOL IN ALBANY.

THROUGH HIS WORK WITH RICHARDSON, WHITE MET THE TWO MEN WHO WOULD BECOME HIS CLOSEST FRIENDS: THE ARCHITECT CHARLES FOLLEN McKIM...

AND THE SCULPTOR AUGUSTUS ST. GAUDENS.

THE THREE YOUNG MEN TOGETHER MADE A GRAND TOUR OF EUROPE IN 1878-79...

WHITE SKETCHING AT EVERY OPPORTUNITY.

HE WAS PROFOUNDLY INSPIRED BY THE ROMANESQUE CHURCHES OF SOUTHERN FRANCE...

AND THE RENAISSANCE STYLES OF ROME AND VENICE, WHICH HE DREAMED OF TRANSPLANTING TO AMERICA.

BACK FROM EUROPE, HE JOINED THE FIRM FOUNDED BY McKIM AND WILLIAM RUTHERFORD MEAD.

McKIM, MEAD AND WHITE WAS BORN. THREE VERY DIFFERENT PERSONALITIES, THOUGH ALWAYS IN TUNE.

IN 1884, WHITE MARRIED BESSIE SPRINGS SMITH, DAUGHTER OF A PROMINENT LONG ISLAND FAMILY.

THREE YEARS LATER, THEIR SON, LAWRENCE GRANT WHITE, WAS BORN.

AS NEW YORK BOOMED IN THE 1880'S, WHITE WAS MUCH IN DEMAND FOR HIS UNERRING TALENT IN ADAPTING HISTORICAL EUROPEAN MOTIFS...

WASHINGTON SQUARE ARCH

JUDSON MEMORIAL CHURCH

THE NEW YORK HERALD BUILDING

ESPECIALLY IN THE ELEGANT HOMES OF THE CITY'S WEALTHIEST FAMILIES...

TIFFANY...VANDERBILT...ASTOR... WHITNEY...STUYVESANT FISH.

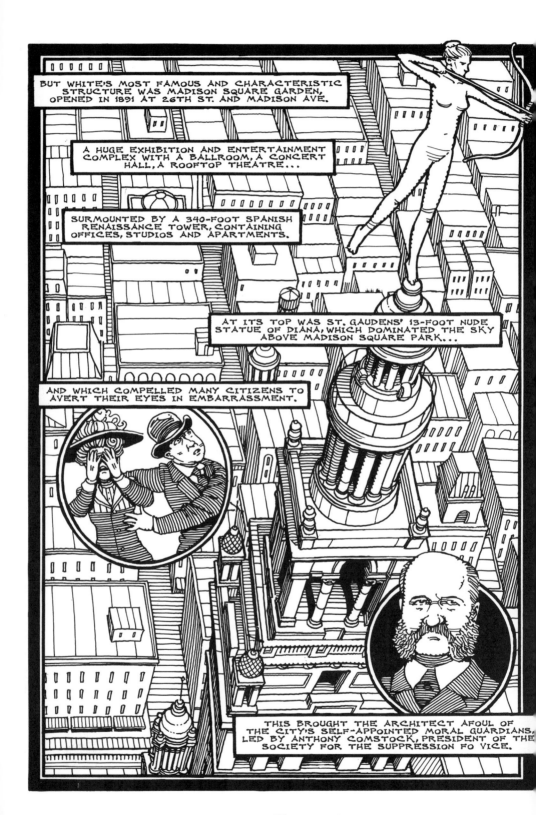

BUT WHITE'S MOST FAMOUS AND CHARACTERISTIC STRUCTURE WAS MADISON SQUARE GARDEN, OPENED IN 1891 AT 26TH ST. AND MADISON AVE.

A HUGE EXHIBITION AND ENTERTAINMENT COMPLEX WITH A BALLROOM, A CONCERT HALL, A ROOFTOP THEATRE...

SURMOUNTED BY A 340-FOOT SPANISH RENAISSANCE TOWER, CONTAINING OFFICES, STUDIOS AND APARTMENTS.

AT ITS TOP WAS ST. GAUDENS' 13-FOOT NUDE STATUE OF DIANA, WHICH DOMINATED THE SKY ABOVE MADISON SQUARE PARK...

AND WHICH COMPELLED MANY CITIZENS TO AVERT THEIR EYES IN EMBARRASSMENT.

THIS BROUGHT THE ARCHITECT AFOUL OF THE CITY'S SELF-APPOINTED MORAL GUARDIANS, LED BY ANTHONY COMSTOCK, PRESIDENT OF THE SOCIETY FOR THE SUPPRESSION FO VICE.

WHITE WAS ALSO A WELL-KNOWN PRESENCE IN THE SOCIAL LIFE OF THE CITY — THE QUINTESSENTIAL "MAN ABOUT TOWN."

GREGARIOUS AND EXUBERANT, FILLED WITH RESTLESS ENERGY, HE CULTIVATED A WIDE CIRCLE OF FRIENDSHIPS AMONG THE CULTURAL AND FINANCIAL ELITE.

HE ALSO HAD AN UNFORTUNATE TASTE FOR YOUNGER WOMEN.

AMONG HIS FRIENDS, HIS FLIRTATIONS WERE NOTORIOUS.

WHILE HIS TOLERANT WIFE BESSIE SPENT HER DAYS AT THE FAMILY'S COUNTRY ESTATE ON LONG ISLAND...

OR AT THEIR CITY RESIDENCE ON GRAMERCY PARK...

"STANNY" MAINTAINED AN APARTMENT IN THE TOWER OF MADISON SQUARE GARDEN...

WHERE HE OFTEN THREW LAVISH PARTIES...

AS WELL AS A PRIVATE STUDIO ON 24TH ST., WHERE HE ENTERTAINED HIS "CONQUESTS"...

EQUIPPED, IT WAS SAID, WITH A RED VELVET SWING.

DESPITE HIS PENCHANT FOR HIGH LIVING, WHITE, UNBEKNOWNST TO MANY, WAS IN DEEP FINANCIAL TROUBLE.

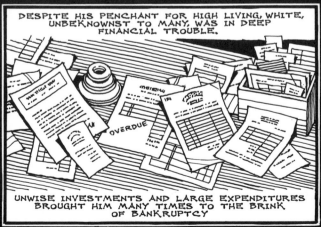

UNWISE INVESTMENTS AND LARGE EXPENDITURES BROUGHT HIM MANY TIMES TO THE BRINK OF BANKRUPTCY

AND WOULD EVENTUALLY CAUSE HIS EXPULSION AS A PARTNER IN HIS OWN FIRM.

IN THE AUTUMN OF 1901, WHITE'S LOVE OF MUSICAL THEATRE — AND THE FEMALE PERFORMERS THEREIN — BROUGHT HIM NIGHT AFTER NIGHT TO THE POPULAR REVUE "FLORADORA"...

THEN IN THE MIDST OF A LONG RUN AT THE CASINO THEATRE ON BROADWAY AT 39TH STREET.

MUSICAL SENSATION "FLORADORA" 14TH WEEK

IN ONE OF THE SHOW'S NUMBERS, A YOUNG "SPANISH DANCER" HAD ALREADY ATTRACTED THE EYE OF MANY A MALE THEATREGOER.

HER NAME, HE DISCOVERED, WAS EVELYN NESBIT...

AND HE SET THE WHEELS IN MOTION TO ARRANGE A MEETING.

PART III

EVELYN

AS THE NEW CENTURY BEGAN, EVELYN NESBIT, AGE 16, WAS
NEWLY ARRIVED IN THE CITY AND ON THE BRINK OF HER
NOTORIOUS CAREER.

FLORENCE EVELYN NESBIT WAS BORN ON CHRISTMAS DAY, 1884, IN TARENTUM, PENNSYLVANIA...

TARENTUM

ALLEGHENY R.

PITTSBURGH

A VILLAGE JUST EAST OF PITTSBURGH.

HER FATHER: WINFIELD SCOTT NESBIT, A MODESTLY SUCCESSFUL ATTORNEY.

HER MOTHER: EVELYN McKENZIE NESBIT.

HER BROTHER, HOWARD, WAS BORN TWO YEARS LATER.

LITTLE FLORENCE WAS HIGH-SPIRITED AND SELF-ASSURED.

HER FATHER ENCOURAGED HER TO READ, SUPPORTED HER INTEREST IN MUSIC AND DANCE.

IN 1895, THE FAMILY RELOCATED TO PITTSBURGH, WHERE MR. NESBIT, AT AGE 40, SUDDENLY DIED.

WIDOW AND CHILDREN WERE PLUNGED INTO POVERTY.

THEY LIVED AND WORKED IN A SERIES OF SHABBY BOARDING HOUSES.

AT TIMES, THE CHILDREN WERE SENT, TOGETHER OR SEPARATELY, TO LIVE WITH VARIOUS RELATIVES...

WHILE MRS. NESBIT SEARCHED FOR EMPLOYMENT AS A SEAMSTRESS OR DRESS DESIGNER.

ALL TOO OFTEN, THE BROTHER AND SISTER FOUND THEIR MOTHER SOBBING HYSTERICALLY.

OH, WHAT WILL BECOME OF US?!

THESE YEARS OF DEPRIVATION WILL HAVE A LASTING EFFECT UPON THE GIRL.

FEELINGS OF ABANDONMENT AND REJECTION WILL NEVER ENTIRELY GO AWAY.

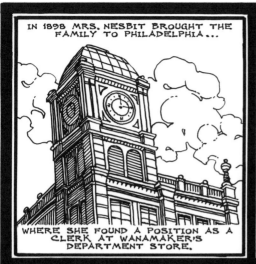

IN 1898 MRS. NESBIT BROUGHT THE FAMILY TO PHILADELPHIA...

WHERE SHE FOUND A POSITION AS A CLERK AT WANAMAKER'S DEPARTMENT STORE.

EVENTUALLY, BOTH CHILDREN WERE GIVEN JOBS AT THE STORE.

FLORENCE WAS A STOCK GIRL AND SOMETIMES WORKED THE COUNTER.

IT WAS NOT LONG BEFORE HER NATURAL ADVANTAGES BECAME EVIDENT.

AT AGE 14, FLORENCE WAS DEVELOPING INTO A BEAUTIFUL YOUNG LADY.

ONE DAY, SHE WAS NOTICED ON THE SIDEWALK BY A LOCAL ILLUSTRATOR.

AND A CAREER AS ARTISTS' MODEL OPENED UP TO HER.

THE YOUNG LADY BECAME MUCH IN DEMAND BY PHILADELPHIA'S PAINTERS AND ILLUSTRATORS...

AND, IN TIME, BY THE CITY'S PHOTOGRAPHERS.

HER INNOCENT VISAGE MADE HER NATURAL FOR ANGELS AND ALLEGORICAL SUBJECTS.

SHE WAS KNOWN AS "LITTLE MISS NESBIT."

THE HOURS SPENT HOLDING A SINGLE POSITION GAVE HER THE COMPOSURE AND INSCRUTABILITY THAT FORMED HER UNIQUE LOOK.

THE NEW AND STEADY INCOME ALLOWED MRS. NESBIT TO LEAVE WANAMAKER'S...

AND TAKE OVER THE MANAGEMENT OF HER DAUGHTER'S CAREER.

IN 1900, THE FAMILY MOVED TO NEW YORK CITY.

THEY LIVED AT FIRST IN A SINGLE ROOM AT 249 WEST 22ND ST.

FLORENCE EVELYN WAS IMMEDIATELY TAKEN UP BY THE CITY'S FINEST PAINTERS AND PHOTOGRAPHERS. (SHE PREFERRED PHOTOGRAPHERS SINCE THEY PAID BETTER AND DID NOT REQUIRE HOURS OF SITTING MOTIONLESS.)

AT THE START OF 1901 SHE HAD JUST TURNED 16, AND SOON HER FACE WAS EVERYWHERE.

THE PUBLIC WONDERED ABOUT HER. PHOTOGRAPHERS CALLED HER THE LITTLE SPHINX. SHE WAS BOTH CHILD AND WOMAN.

CHARLES DANA GIBSON DEPICTED HER AS "THE ETERNAL QUESTION."

TO THE EXTENT THAT SHE WAS AMBITIOUS AT ALL, EVELYN, AS SHE NOW CALLED HERSELF, WANTED TO BE ON THE STAGE.

IN MAY OF 1901, SHE WAS HIRED TO JOIN THE CAST OF "FLORADORA."

AS THE "SPANISH DANCER" SHE EXCITED THE INTEREST OF THOSE MEN WHO CAME NIGHT AFTER NIGHT TO APPRAISE THE FEMALE PERFORMERS.

AT FIRST, MRS. NESBIT OBJECTED, BUT THE GIRL'S APPEAL WAS OBVIOUS.

SOMEHOW, HER AGE WAS OVERLOOKED.

THE OTHER GIRLS OF THE CHORUS WERE EVELYN'S FIRST REAL FRIENDS.

MOST OF THEM HOPED TO "SNAG" WEALTHY HUSBANDS.

FLOWERS ARRIVED BACKSTAGE NIGHTLY...

AND THE "STAGE DOOR JOHNNIES" AWAITED OUTSIDE.

AMONG HER MANY ADMIRERS WAS THE MILLIONAIRE BANKER JAMES GARLAND.

ALTHOUGH MARRIED AND IN HIS 60'S, HE ATTENDED EVELYN WITH PARTICULAR VIGOR.

HE TREATED HER AND HER MOTHER TO WEEKEND YACHTING EXCURSIONS ALONG THE HUDSON RIVER.

EVELYN KEPT AN ACTIVE SCHEDULE, POSING DURING THE DAY AND DANCING ONSTAGE AT NIGHT.

ONE DAY IN SEPTEMBER OF 1901, SHE WAS INVITED TO LUNCH BY ONE OF HER CHUMS IN THE CHORUS, TO MEET SOME "SOCIETY FRIENDS."

THEIR DESTINATION, HOWEVER, WAS NOT ONE OF THE CITY'S FINER RESTAURANTS...

BUT A NONDESCRIPT BUILDING AT 22 WEST 24TH STREET. ON THE GROUND FLOOR WAS THE TOY EMPORIUM OF F.A.O. SCHWARZ.

THEY ENTERED THROUGH A SIDE DOOR AND CLIMBED A FLIGHT OF STAIRS.

WAITING AT THE TOP WAS THE TOWERING RED-HAIRED ARCHITECT STANFORD WHITE.

HIS PRIVATE STUDIO WAS LINED WITH RED VELVET, FILLED WITH FINE PAINTINGS AND ANTIQUE FURNITURE.

A SECOND GENTLEMAN JOINED THEM FOR THE ELABORATE LUNCH, WHICH WAS DELIVERED FROM DELMONICO'S

EVELYN TASTED HER FIRST GLASS OF CHAMPAGNE.

AFTERWARD, WHITE USHERED THE LADIES TO AN UPSTAIRS ROOM, WHERE A RED VELVET SWING HUNG FROM THE CEILING.

THEY TOOK TURNS BEING PUSHED BY THE ARCHITECT...

ALL OF IT QUITE CAREFREE AND INNOCENT.

AFTER THAT DAY, WHITE BECAME A KIND OF BENEVOLENT FATHER FIGURE TO EVELYN AND HER FAMILY.

HE CULTIVATED AND CHARMED MRS. NESBIT AND CONVINCED HER THAT HE HAD NOTHING BUT THE MOST PROTECTIVE OF INTENTIONS.

HE SECURED, FOR THE FAMILY, ROOMS AT THE AUDUBON HOTEL ACROSS BROADWAY FROM THE CASINO THEATRE...

AND LATER MOVED THEM INTO A PERSONALLY DESIGNED SUITE AT THE WELLINGTON HOTEL, ON 7TH AVENUE.

HE PAID FOR A PRIVATE SCHOOL FOR YOUNG HOWARD...

AND HAD EVELYN'S TEETH, TWO OF WHICH WERE SLIGHTLY DISCOLORED, REPAIRED BY HIS PERSONAL DENTIST.

AFTER SEVERAL MORE LUNCHES, EVELYN FOUND HERSELF MUCH ATTRACTED TO THE CHARISMATIC OLDER MAN.

TO HER, HE WAS UNFAILINGLY KIND GENEROUS AND ATTENTIVE.

HE BROUGHT HER TO ELEGANT PARTIES AT HIS MADISON SQUARE GARDEN APARTMENT, WHERE SHE MINGLED WITH THE ELITE OF MUSIC, ART, FINANCE, AND POLITICS.

WHITE WOULD SOMETIMES ESCORT HER TO THE VERY TOP OF THE TOWER...

WHERE SHE COULD REACH UP AND TOUCH THE FOOT OF DIANA...

THE CITY SPREAD BELOW HER.

BUT IT WAS NOT LONG BEFORE "STANNY'S" TRUE INTENTIONS REVEALED THEMSELVES.

IN NOVEMBER, HE ARRANGED FOR MRS. NESBIT TO VISIT RELATIVES IN PITTSBURGH...

AND ONE NIGHT INVITED EVELYN, AFTER THE PERFORMANCE OF "FLORADORA," TO HIS 24TH STREET ROOMS.

SHE THOUGHT IT ODD, AT FIRST, THAT NO ONE ELSE WAS THERE.

BUT SHE FELT PERFECTLY SAFE WITH THE OLDER MAN.

THEY ENJOYED A FINE MEAL AND DRANK MUCH CHAMPAGNE.

AFTER DINNER, AS EVELYN WILL DESCRIBE IT YEARS LATER, HE GUIDED HER UP A NARROW BACK STAIRWAY...

TO A SMALL ROOM CROWDED WITH PAINTINGS AND STATUARY.

BEHIND A TAPESTRY WAS AN EXOTIC BEDROOM, LINED WITH MIRRORS AND ILLUMINATED SUBTLY BY INDIRECT COLORED LIGHTS.

ANOTHER GLASS OF CHAMPAGNE— WAS IT DRUGGED?

AND EVELYN PASSED OUT.

SHE WILL REMEMBER NOTHING UNTIL WAKING UP SOMETIME LATER IN WHITE'S BED. SHE WAS NAKED, AND THE ARCHITECT WAS LYING NAKED BESIDE HER!

SHE KNEW AT ONCE WHAT HAD HAPPENED. SHE COULD FEEL IT. SHE HAD BEEN VIOLATED!

SHE SCREAMED AND CRIED, WHILE THE FLUSTERED OLDER MAN TRIED TO COMFORT HER.

HE WARNED HER TO TELL NO ONE.

EVELYN RETURNED TO HER HOTEL IN A STATE OF INSENSIBILITY...

AND REMAINED IN A STUPOR FOR SEVERAL DAYS.

BUT WHITE CONTINUED HIS ATTENTIONS, AND EVELYN REMAINED DRAWN TO HIM.

TO HER HE WAS "A FORCE OF NATURE." TO HIM SHE WAS "THE PERFECT PRIZE."

HIS PET NAME FOR HER WAS "KITTENS."

THEY CARRIED ON A DISCREET LOVE AFFAIR WHILE OUTWARDLY HE PLAYED THE ROLE OF PROTECTOR AND BENEFACTOR.

SHE WAS INTRODUCED TO A LIFE OF LUXURY AND PLEASURE.

HE COMPLETELY TOOK OVER HER EDUCATION, CULTURAL, SOCIAL— AND SEXUAL.

BUT INEVITABLY THEIR ASSIOCIATION BEGAN TO LOSE ITS INTENSITY.

BY THE DAWN OF 1902, EVELYN HAD ACCEPTED THE REALITY THAT WHITE TRULY LOVED HIS WIFE AND WOULD NEVER LEAVE HIS FAMILY...

WHILE HIS EYE CONTINUED TO BE DRAWN TO NEWER AND YOUNGER "PRIZES."

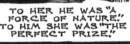

IN APRIL, "FLORADORA" ENDED ITS RUN, AND EVELYN ACCEPTED A FEATURED ROLE IN A NEW MUSICAL REVUE, "THE WILD ROSE."

SHE ALSO BEGAN TO ACCEPT LUNCHEON AND DINNER INVITATIONS FROM THE WOULD-BE SUITORS WHO CONTINUED TO SWARM THE STAGE DOOR.

ONE YOUNG MAN WHO PRESSED HIS ATTENTIONS WAS 20-YEAR-OLD JACK BARRYMORE, YOUNGEST OF THE FAMED ACTING SIBLINGS...

ETHEL

LIONEL

AT THAT TIME PURSUING A CAREER AS A NEWSPAPER CARTOONIST.

THEY BEGAN AN INTENSE BUT CHASTE LOVE AFFAIR THAT WAS GOSSIPED ABOUT IN THE NEWSPAPERS.

IN TIME, THEY TALKED OF MARRIAGE.

BUT MRS. NESBIT THOUGHT BARRYMORE A WASTREL AND DISAPPROVED OF THE ROMANCE.

SHE ENLISTED STANFORD WHITE TO QUASH IT.

AT A MEETING IN THE NESBITS' HOTEL SUITE, THE ARCHITECT QUIZZED THE YOUNG MAN AS TO HIS INTENTIONS.

WHAT WILL YOU LIVE ON?

WE'LL LIVE ON LOVE.

35

IN SHORT ORDER, ARRANGEMENTS WERE MADE TO WITHDRAW EVELYN FROM HER MODELING AND THEATRICAL CAREERS...

AND ENROLL HER AT AN ALL-GIRL PRIVATE BOARDING SCHOOL: THE DEMILLE SCHOOL IN POMPTON LAKES, NEW JERSEY.

EVELYN RESISTED BEING YANKED FROM HER GLAMOROUS LIFE IN NEW YORK, BUT AT AGE 17 THERE WAS LITTLE SHE COULD DO.

AND SOON SHE FELL OBEDIENTLY INTO THE ACADEMIC ROUTINE...

INTERRUPTED OCCASIONALLY BY VISITS FROM JOURNALISTS...

AND FROM STANFORD WHITE, STILL KEEPING A FATHERLY EYE UPON HER.

IT WAS AT THIS TIME THAT ONE OF HER NEW YORK ADMIRERS RENEWED HIS PURSUIT.

DURING THE RUNS OF "FLORADORA" AND "THE WILD ROSE," HE HAD FLOODED HER WITH FLOWERS AND LETTERS.

WHEN THEY HAD FIRST MET SHE COULD SEE THE "MADNESS" IN HIS EYES.

PART IV

HARRY

IN 1901, WHEN HE FIRST LAID EYES ON EVELYN NESBIT, HARRY K. THAW, AGE 30, HAD THE MEANS TO INDULGE HIS EVERY DESIRE.

HE WAS BORN FEBRUARY 12, 1871, IN PITTSBURGH, THIRD OF FIVE CHILDREN BORN TO WILLIAM K. THAW, WHO MADE THE FAMILY'S FORTUNE IN STEEL, COKE AND RAILROADS...

AND MARY COPLEY THAW.

HIS BROTHERS: JOSIAH AND EDWARD
HIS SISTERS: MARGARET AND ALICE.

HARRY GREW UP SPOILED AND PETTED BY HIS ADORING MOTHER.

BUT HE WAS A "NERVOUS" CHILD...

PRONE TO TANTRUMS AND EPISODES OF "EXCITEMENT"...

TO SUCH A DEGREE THAT SHE FEARED HE MIGHT HAVE INHERITED THE STRAINS OF INSANITY THAT RAN THROUGH BOTH SIDES OF THE FAMILY.

HARRY'S CHILDHOOD WAS SPENT AT THE FAMILY'S MANSION:

"LYNDHURST" ON BEECHWOOD BLVD. IN PITTSBURGH.

AS A YOUTH HE MADE SEVERAL TOURS OF EUROPE WITH HIS MOTHER AND SIBLINGS.

HE ATTENDED WOOSTER PREP SCHOOL AND THEN THE UNIVERSITY OF PITTSBURGH...

BUT HE DISPLAYED MORE INTEREST IN POKER, LIQUOR, AND WOMEN THAN IN ACADEMIC PURSUITS.

AFTER A BRIEF TERM AT HARVARD, HE WAS EXPELLED FOR "IMMORAL PRACTICES."

IN TRUTH, ALL HE WANTED TO BE WAS A RICH IDLER...

THUS DISPLEASING THE ELDER THAW, WHO, UPON HIS PASSING, LEFT HARRY WITH A MONTHLY ALLOWANCE OF A MERE $2500.

HIS MOTHER SOON RAISED THE AMOUNT TO $80,000.

HARRY WORKED TO ESTABLISH AN UNSAVORY REPUTATION FOR HIMSELF IN THE UNITED STATES AND THE CAPITALS OF EUROPE.

HE THREW LAVISH PARTIES AND DINNERS.

HE ONCE DROVE AN AUTOMOBILE THROUGH A FIFTH AVENUE STORE WINDOW.

HE CHASED A CAB DRIVER, WHOM HE THOUGHT HAD CHEATED HIM, WITH A SHOTGUN.

HE RODE A HORSE INTO A NEW YORK MEN'S CLUB WHICH HAD DENIED HIM MEMBERSHIP.

DARKER RUMORS ABOUNDED:

POSING AS "MR. REID," A THEATRICAL COACH, HE WOULD RENT CHEAP ROOMS TO WHICH HE WOULD LURE YOUNG ASPIRING ACTRESSES.

HE WOULD THEN BIND AND WHIP THEM.

AT LEAST ONE HE FORCED INTO A BATHTUB AND POURED SCALDING WATER OVER HER...

ALL OF THIS IN THE GUISE OF A GALLANT PROTECTOR OF FEMALE VIRTUE.

EARLY ON, HE ALLIED HIMSELF WITH ANTHONY COMSTOCK, IN THE ONGOING CRUSADE AGAINST VICE...

AND NURTURED AN ESPECIAL HATRED FOR THAT SATANIC DEFILER OF WOMEN...

STANFORD WHITE.

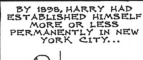

BY 1898, HARRY HAD ESTABLISHED HIMSELF MORE OR LESS PERMANENTLY IN NEW YORK CITY...

IN ROOMS AT THE KNICKERBOCKER HOTEL, ACCOMPANIED BY HIS LONG-SUFFERING MANSERVANT BEDFORD.

HE ATTENDED THE THEATRE REGULARLY, THE BETTER TO FIND YOUNG LADIES IN NEED OF RESCUE.

SOMETIME IN THE FALL OF 1901, HE FIRST WONDERED ABOUT THE BEAUTIFUL SPANISH DANCER IN THE CAST OF "FLORADORA."

HE WATCHED HER FOR A SOLID MONTH FROM HIS BOX AT THE CASINO THEATRE, AND DID THE SAME WHEN SHE APPEARED IN "THE WILD ROSE."

BY THEN, HE HAD HEARD THE GOSSIP ABOUT EVELYN NESBIT'S "SPECIAL" RELATIONSHIP WITH STANFORD WHITE.

HE BEGAN TO ENTREAT HER WITH FLOWERS, GIFTS, EVEN CASH...

AND WITH LETTERS MYSTERIOUSLY SIGNED "MR. MUNROE."

FINALLY, ACCOMPANIED BY A FRIEND, SHE MET HIM FOR LUNCH AT RECTOR'S RESTAURANT ON BROADWAY AT 44TH STREET.

THERE, BETWEEN HIS EXCITED MONOLOGUES, HE DROPPED TO HIS KNEES, KISSED HER SKIRT, AND CONFESSED HIS TRUE IDENTITY.

I AM NOT MR. MUNROE, I AM HARRY K. THAW OF PITTSBURGH.

YOU'VE HEARD OF ME?

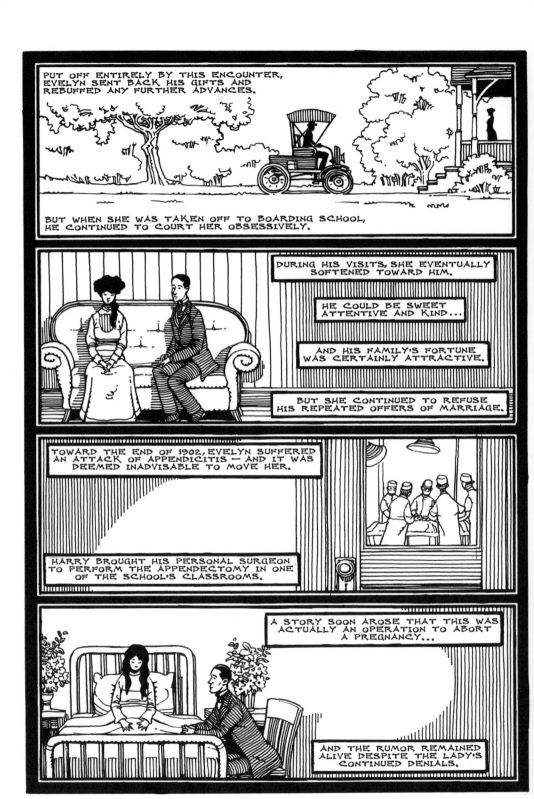

PUT OFF ENTIRELY BY THIS ENCOUNTER, EVELYN SENT BACK HIS GIFTS AND REBUFFED ANY FURTHER ADVANCES.

BUT WHEN SHE WAS TAKEN OFF TO BOARDING SCHOOL, HE CONTINUED TO COURT HER OBSESSIVELY.

DURING HIS VISITS, SHE EVENTUALLY SOFTENED TOWARD HIM.

HE COULD BE SWEET ATTENTIVE AND KIND...

AND HIS FAMILY'S FORTUNE WAS CERTAINLY ATTRACTIVE.

BUT SHE CONTINUED TO REFUSE HIS REPEATED OFFERS OF MARRIAGE.

TOWARD THE END OF 1902, EVELYN SUFFERED AN ATTACK OF APPENDICITIS — AND IT WAS DEEMED INADVISABLE TO MOVE HER.

HARRY BROUGHT HIS PERSONAL SURGEON TO PERFORM THE APPENDECTOMY IN ONE OF THE SCHOOL'S CLASSROOMS.

A STORY SOON AROSE THAT THIS WAS ACTUALLY AN OPERATION TO ABORT A PREGNANCY...

AND THE RUMOR REMAINED ALIVE DESPITE THE LADY'S CONTINUED DENIALS.

EARLY IN THE NEW YEAR, HARRY, WHO HAD MANAGED TO WIN OVER MRS. NESBIT, SUGGESTED AN OCEAN VOYAGE AND A TOUR OF EUROPE TO AID IN EVELYN'S RECOVERY.

IN MAY OF 1903, SHE AND HER MOTHER DEPARTED FOR ENGLAND. HARRY FOLLOWED ON A SEPARATE SHIP.

IN LONDON AND PARIS, THEY STAYED IN SEPARATE HOTELS.

HARRY WAS ON HIS BEST BEHAVIOR.

ALL THE WHILE, HE PRESSED EVELYN TO MARRY HIM, AND SHE KEPT REFUSING.

I CANNOT MARRY YOU!

EVENTUALLY, IN A PARIS HOTEL ROOM, SHE MADE "THE BIGGEST MISTAKE OF MY LIFE" AND TOLD HIM THE STORY OF HER SEDUCTION AND RUINATION BY STANFORD WHITE.

THEY STAYED UP ALL NIGHT, AS HARRY PRESSED HER FOR DETAILS. HE REACTED WITH HYSTERICAL TEARS, AND PACED THE FLOOR IN AGITATION.

BEFORE LONG, A GROWING TENSION BETWEEN HARRY AND MRS. NESBIT RESULTED IN HER RETURN TO LONDON...

AND, EVENTUALLY, TO AMERICA.

TO MAINTAIN APPEARANCES, HE HIRED A LADY AS CHAPERONE.

AND HE AND EVELYN CONTINUED THEIR TOUR OF THE CONTINENT: GERMANY, THE NETHERLANDS, AUSTRIA.

IN AUSTRIA, HE RENTED AN ENTIRE CASTLE HIGH IN THE MOUNTAINS: SCHLOSS-KATZENSTEIN.

THEY OCCUPIED SEPARATE ROOMS.

HERE, ONE TERRIFYING NIGHT, HE BURST INTO HER ROOM, NAKED AND IN A FURY.

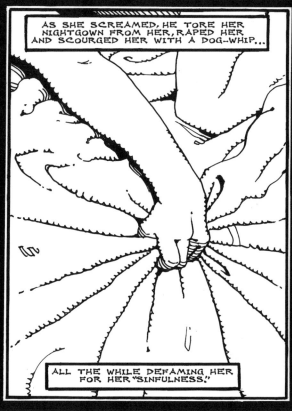

AS SHE SCREAMED, HE TORE HER NIGHTGOWN FROM HER, RAPED HER AND SCOURGED HER WITH A DOG-WHIP...

ALL THE WHILE DEFAMING HER FOR HER "SINFULNESS."

FOR THE REMAINDER OF THEIR THREE WEEKS AT THE CASTLE, EVELYN REFUSED TO LEAVE HER ROOM.

AFTER THAT, THEY CONTINUED THEIR JOURNEY: TO SWITZERLAND AND BACK TO PARIS...

HARRY BEHAVING AS IF NOTHING HAD HAPPENED, EVELYN ALTERNATELY SILENT AND SOBBING.

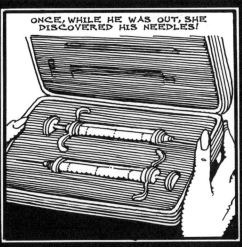

ONCE, WHILE HE WAS OUT, SHE DISCOVERED HIS NEEDLES!

IN OCTOBER, EVELYN RETURNED ALONE TO NEW YORK.

HARRY CAME SOME WEEKS LATER.

SHE SECLUDED HERSELF AT DIFFERENT HOTELS...

AND QUIETLY TRIED TO RESUME HER MODELING AND STAGE CAREERS.

DURING THIS TIME, SHE RESISTED SEEKING OUT "STANNY."

BUT AFTER A CHANCE ENCOUNTER ON THE STREET, HE TELEPHONED HER.

BY THIS TIME, EVELYN'S MOTHER HAD ALLIED HERSELF WITH THE ARCHITECT TO WREST HER DAUGHTER FROM THE INFLUENCE OF HARRY THAW.

WHITE HAD CONTINUED HIS FINANCIAL SUPPORT OF MRS. NESBIT AND HOWARD, NOW AGE 15.

WHITE AND OTHERS FILLED EVELYN IN ON HARRY'S DECADENT HISTORY...

INCLUDING HIS ADDICTIONS TO BOTH COCAINE AND MORPHINE.

ONE DAY IN NOVEMBER, WHITE BROUGHT EVELYN TO THE OFFICE OF AN ATTORNEY, A MISSHAPEN MAN NAMED ABE HUMMEL.

FROM HER, THE LAWYER TOOK A DETAILED DEPOSITION, LAYING OUT THAW'S MANIA AND CRUELTY DURING THEIR EUROPEAN EXCURSION.

WHEN HARRY RETURNED TO THE CITY, HE RENEWED HIS COURTSHIP WITH EVEN GREATER ZEAL...

AND EVELYN, WHO HAD LITTLE KNOWLEDGE OF WHAT WOULD CONSTITUTE A "NORMAL" LOVE AFFAIR, SLOWLY RESPONDED TO HIS SINCERE AND ERNEST ENTREATIES.

IN THE SPRING OF 1904, THEY MADE ANOTHER TOUR OF EUROPE, THIS TIME WITH NO OUTRAGEOUS EPISODES.

SHE AT LAST GAVE IN TO HIS REPEATED PROPOSALS, AND THEY WERE MARRIED ON APRIL 5, 1905...

THE BRIDE: AGE 20.

THE GROOM: 34.

IN A SMALL CEREMONY AT THE HOME OF REV. McEWAN, OF THE THIRD PRESBYTERIAN CHURCH IN PITTSBURGH.

THE BRIDE'S MOTHER, WHO HAD BY THEN WASHED HER HANDS OF HER WAYWARD DAUGHTER AND REMARRIED, ATTENDED WITH HER HUSBAND, CHARLES HOLMAN.

THE NEWLYWEDS DEPARTED FOR A HONEYMOON TRIP TO ARIZONA AND CALIFORNIA.

THE COUPLE THEN SETTLED INTO AN UNEASY DOMESTIC LIFE AT "LYNDHURST."

THERE WAS NO LOVE LOST BETWEEN THE BRIDE AND THE FORMIDABLE MOTHER THAW...

WHO HAD OPPOSED THE MATCH FROM THE BEGINNING.

LIKEWISE HARRY'S SISTERS: ALICE, WHO HAD MARRIED AN IMPOVERISHED NOBLEMAN, THE EARL OF YARMOUTH

AND MARGARET, WHO WAS WED TO GEORGE CARNEGIE, NEPHEW OF THE STEEL MAGNATE.

AFTER THE EXCITEMENT OF BROADWAY AND EUROPE, EVELYN FOUND LIFE AT "LYNDHURST" EXCRUCIATINGLY MONOTONOUS, FILLED WITH CHURCH WORK AND DOMESTIC CHATTER.

PITTSBURGH SOCIETY WOULD NOT RECEIVE HER.

TO THE FAMILY'S EMBARRASSMENT, A SERIES OF SENSUOUS PHOTOGRAPHS SHE HAD POSED FOR YEARS EARLIER MADE THEIR WAY INTO A LOCAL NEWSPAPER.

HARRY, INITIALLY ATTENTIVE, SPENT MORE AND MORE TIME AWAY FROM HOME.

MARRIAGE DID NOT SOFTEN HARRY'S RAGE AND RESENTMENT TOWARD STANFORD WHITE.

HE CONTINUED TO PESTER EVELYN FOR DETAILS OF HER RELATIONSHIP WITH THE ARCHITECT.

SHE SURRENDERED THE LETTERS THAT HER SEDUCER HAD WRITTEN TO HER.

HARRY RESUMED HIS CAMPAIGN TO EXPOSE HIM AND THOSE PRIVILEGED MEN OF HIS CIRCLE.

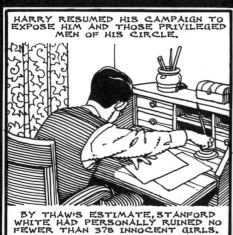

BY THAW'S ESTIMATE, STANFORD WHITE HAD PERSONALLY RUINED NO FEWER THAN 378 INNOCENT GIRLS.

HE HIRED DETECTIVES TO FOLLOW THE MAN'S EVERY MOVEMENT...

AS WELL AS THOSE OF EVELYN.

HE CLAIMED THAT WHITE, IN TURN, HAD HIRED CRIMINALS FROM THE NOTORIOUS MONK EASTMAN GANG TO FOLLOW AND ELIMINATE HIM.

HE PURCHASED A PISTOL AND PRACTICED WITH IT ON THE GROUNDS OF "LYNDHURST."

HARRY SENT EVELYN TO HIS PERSONAL DENTIST, TO HAVE THE WORK THAT WHITE HAD PAID FOR REVERSED.

HE NEXT CAME UP WITH THE IDEA THAT HIS WIFE SHOULD NEVER AGAIN UTTER THE ARCHITECT'S NAME.

SHE WILL ONLY REFER TO HIM AS "THE BEAST" OR SIMPLY AS "THE B," WHICH CAN ALSO STAND FOR "THE BOUNDER" OR "THE BLACKGUARD."

EARLY IN 1906, HARRY DECIDED THAT ANOTHER TOUR OF EUROPE WAS IN ORDER.

IN JUNE, PREPARATORY TO THEIR DEPARTURE, THEY CAME TO NEW YORK.

MOTHER THAW WHO WOULD ACCOMPANY THEM IN EUROPE, HAD SET SAIL ON AN EARLIER VESSEL.

THEY TOOK A SUITE AT THE HOTEL LORRAINE, FIFTH AVENUE AT 49TH STREET.

HARRY SPENT HIS DAYS WITH HIS MALE CRONIES, WHILE EVELYN SHOPPED ALONG FIFTH AVENUE...

FOLLOWED AT A DISCREET DISTANCE BY HER HUSBAND'S DETECTIVES.

PART V

THE FATAL NIGHT

MONDAY, JUNE 25, 1906,
IS OPPRESSIVELY HOT AND MUGGY.

NEW YORKERS, SEEKING RELIEF, HAVE NO INKLING OF THE
DRAMA THAT WILL PLAY OUT THIS EVENING AT MADISON
SQUARE GARDEN.

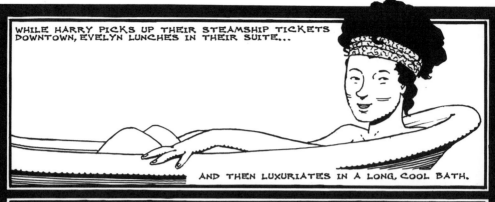

WHILE HARRY PICKS UP THEIR STEAMSHIP TICKETS DOWNTOWN, EVELYN LUNCHES IN THEIR SUITE...

AND THEN LUXURIATES IN A LONG, COOL BATH.

132

IN THE EVENING, HARRY BECOMES IMPATIENT WITH HIS WIFE'S PREPARATIONS AND GOES OUT ALONE.

AT ABOUT 7:00PM, EVELYN MEETS HER HUSBAND IN THE BAR AT SHERRY'S RESTAURANT, NEAR THEIR HOTEL AT FIFTH AVENUE AND 44TH STREET.

JOINING THEM IS A JOURNALIST FRIEND OF HARRY'S, TRUXTON BEALE.

SHE FINDS IT ODD THAT HARRY WEARS A HEAVY OVERCOAT, WHICH HE DECLINES TO REMOVE IN THE STIFLING HEAT.

THEY DECIDE UPON DINNER AT CAFE MARTIN, ON 26TH STREET BETWEEN BROADWAY AND FIFTH AVENUE...

A POPULAR GATHERING SPOT FOR THE THEATRE CROWD.

THEY ARRIVE THROUGH THE 26TH ST. ENTRANCE AND ARE SHOWN TO A TABLE IN THE MAIN DOWNSTAIRS DINING ROOM.

HERE, THEY ARE MET BY THEIR OTHER COMPANION FOR THE EVENING: TOMMY McCALEB, AND OLD FAMILY FRIEND OF THE THAWS.

EVELYN, FACING THE RESTAURANT'S FIFTH AVENUE ENTRANCE, SUDDENLY BECOMES NERVOUS AND APPREHENSIVE...

FOR ENTERING THE ESTABLISHMENT IS NONE OTHER THAN STANFORD WHITE.

THE ARCHITECT HAS SPENT THE DAY IN HIS USUAL FLURRY OF ACTIVITY.

IN THE AFTERNOON, HE WATCHES THE FINAL RUN-THROUGH OF THE MUSICAL REVUE "MAMZELLE CHAMPAGNE"...

WHICH WILL PREMIERE TONIGHT AT MADISON SQUARE GARDEN'S ROOFTOP THEATRE.

HE ASKS THE STAGE MANAGER IF AN INTRODUCTION MIGHT BE ARRANGED TO A PARTICULAR CHORUS GIRL WHO HAS ATTRACTED HIS EYE.

LATER IN THE DAY, WHITE MEETS HIS SON, LAWRENCE, AN ARCHITECTURE STUDENT ON A VISIT HOME, WITH A FRIEND, FROM HARVARD.

THEY DECIDE UPON DINNER AT CAFE MARTIN BEFORE ATTENDING THE THEATRE.

ENTERING FROM THE FIFTH AVENUE SIDE, THE PARTY PASSES THROUGH THE MAIN DINING ROOM BEFORE GOING UPSTAIRS TO THE SMALLER EUROPEAN-STYLE CAFE.

IF WHITE NOTICES EVELYN AND HARRY, HE GIVES NO INDICATION OF IT.

HARRY, HIS BACK TO THE RESTAURANT, HAS APPARENTLY NOT NOTICED WHITE'S ENTRANCE.

EVELYN CONTEMPLATES NOT TELLING HIM, BUT THINKS BETTER OF IT AND PASSES HIM A NOTE:

HARRY IS GREATLY ANGERED AT HAVING MISSED HIS NEMESIS.

THE PARTY QUICKLY FINISHES DINNER AND LEAVES THE RESTAURANT.

THEY THEN WALK THE TWO BLOCKS TO MADISON SQUARE GARDEN, WHERE THEY HAVE TICKETS FOR THE OPENING NIGHT OF "MAMZELLE CHAMPAGNE."

EVELYN THINKS THIS CHOICE OF ENTERTAINMENT ODD, SINCE HER HUSBAND USUALLY AVOIDS ANY LOCATION ASSOCIATED WITH "THE B."

THE PARTY ENTERS THE OPEN-AIR THEATRE AT ABOUT 9:00PM, THE SHOW ALREADY IN PROGRESS...

AND ARE SHOWN TO WHAT HARRY CALLS "ROTTEN SEATS" SOME DISTANCE FROM THE STAGE.

THE THEATRE IS SET UP AS AN INFORMAL NIGHT-CLUB IN WHICH PATRONS MAY CIRCULATE AMONG THE TABLES.

HARRY SEEMS MORE THAN USUALLY AGITATED.

AND THEN STARTS THE PROCESS ANEW...

FOR A TIME, HE SITS WITH THE FINANCIER JAMES CLINCH SMITH, BROTHER-IN-LAW, IRONICALLY, OF STANFORD WHITE.

HE GETS UP FROM THE TABLE, PACES ABOUT THE ROOM, AND SITS DOWN AGAIN...

ALL THE TIME WEARING HIS STRAW BOATER AND HEAVY OVERCOAT.

AT ABOUT 11:00PM, WHITE ENTERS THE THEATRE AND PROCEEDS ALONE TO HIS FRONT ROW TABLE. (LAWRENCE AND HIS FRIEND HAVE GONE TO A DIFFERENT SHOW.)

THERE IS A SMALL COMMOTION IN THE AUDIENCE, AS PEOPLE ACKNOWLEDGE HIS PRESENCE.

EVELYN IS STRUCK WITH FEAR, BUT HARRY, BACK AT THE TABLE, DOES NOT SEEM TO HAVE NOTICED THE ARCHITECT'S ARRIVAL.

EVELYN SUGGESTS THAT THEY LEAVE. EVERYONE IS AGREEABLE, AND THE PARTY WALKS TOWARD THE ELEVATORS.

SHE IS ALMOST INSIDE WHEN SHE LOOKS BACK... WHERE IS HARRY?

THE SOLOIST ONSTAGE, BACKED BY A CHORUS OF LOVELY LADIES, SINGS "I COULD LOVE A MILLION GIRLS."

SUDDENLY, HARRY IS STANDING AT WHITE'S TABLE.

THE ARCHITECT MAKES A MOVE TO RISE, AND, FROM TWO FEET AWAY, THAW FIRES TWICE, DIRECTLY INTO THE MAN'S FACE.

A THIRD SHOT ENTERS HIS SHOULDER.

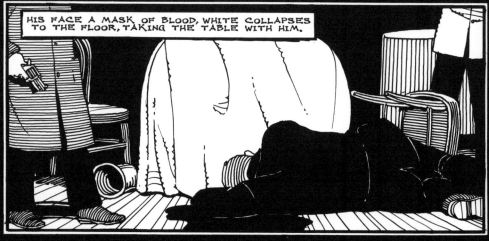

HIS FACE A MASK OF BLOOD, WHITE COLLAPSES TO THE FLOOR, TAKING THE TABLE WITH HIM.

AT FIRST, THE THEATRE IS STUNNED INTO SILENCE. A MOMENT LATER, ALL IS CHAOS.

THE STAGE MANAGER ORDERS THE PLAYERS TO CONTINUE THEIR NUMBER, BUT ALL OF THEM FLEE THE STAGE.

HARRY MAKES NO ATTEMPT TO ESCAPE. HOLDING THE REVOLVER ALOFT, HE EMPTIES THE REMAINING BULLETS.

I DID IT BECAUSE HE RUINED MY WIFE! HE HAD IT COMING TO HIM!

A NEW YORK CITY FIREMAN, PAUL BRUDI, HAPPENS TO BE PRESENT. HE TAKES THE ASSAILANT INTO CUSTODY.

EVELYN AND HER HUSBAND MEET IN THE ELEVATOR.

OH, HARRY, WHAT HAVE YOU DONE?

IT'S ALL RIGHT DEAR. I HAVE PROBABLY SAVED YOUR LIFE.

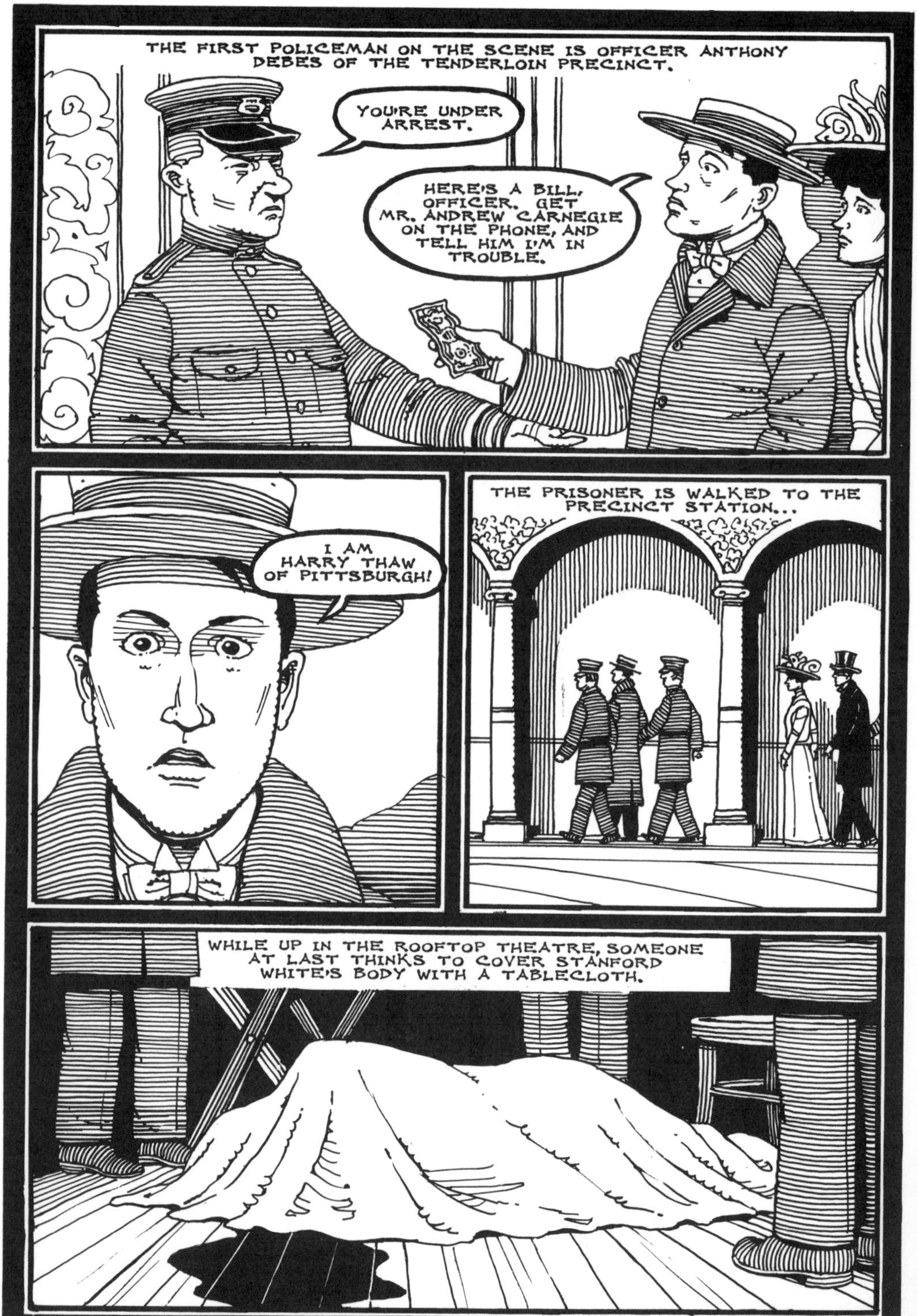
THE FIRST POLICEMAN ON THE SCENE IS OFFICER ANTHONY DEBES OF THE TENDERLOIN PRECINCT.
YOU'RE UNDER ARREST.
HERE'S A BILL, OFFICER. GET MR. ANDREW CARNEGIE ON THE PHONE, AND TELL HIM I'M IN TROUBLE.
I AM HARRY THAW OF PITTSBURGH!
THE PRISONER IS WALKED TO THE PRECINCT STATION...
WHILE UP IN THE ROOFTOP THEATRE, SOMEONE AT LAST THINKS TO COVER STANFORD WHITE'S BODY WITH A TABLECLOTH.

PART VI
TRIALS AND TRIBULATIONS

CRIMINAL COURT
BUILDING

THE WHEELS OF THE JUSTICE SYSTEM GRIND TO A
RESOLUTION UNSATISFACTORY TO EVERYONE CONCERNED.

THE MURDER IS A WINDFALL FOR NEW YORK'S NEWSPAPERS, WHICH KEEP IT IN THE HEADLINES DAILY.

"THE ROOFTOP MURDER," A MOVING PICTURE FROM EDISON'S STUDIO, IS IN THE NICKELODEONS WITHIN A WEEK OF THE TRAGEDY.

THURSDAY, JUNE 28
THE BODY OF STANFORD WHITE IS TRANSPORTED TO ST. JAMES, LONG ISLAND, FOR A FUNERAL SERVICE AT THE TOWN'S EPISCOPAL CHURCH...

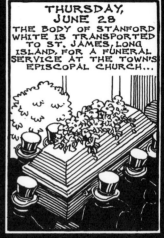

AND IS LAID TO REST IN THE ADJOINING GRAVEYARD.

IN THE MEANTIME, HARRY THAW OCCUPIES A CELL AT THE CITY PRISON IN DOWNTOWN MANHATTAN — KNOWN AS "THE TOMBS."

BUT HE DOES NOT EXACTLY LANGUISH.

HE ENTERTAINS VISITORS, ENJOYS MEALS FROM DELMONICO'S, GIVES INTERVIEWS TO ANY AND ALL JOURNALISTS.

HE DISPLAYS NO REMORSE FOR HIS ACT. IN FACT...

I BELIEVE THE COMMUNITY OWES ME A DEBT OF THANKS.

IN THE OUTSIDE WORLD, AS WHITE'S SCANDALOUS EXPLOITS ARE EXPOSED TO THE READING PUBLIC, SYMPATHY FALLS DECIDEDLY ON THE KILLER'S SIDE.

IT SEEMS THAT THE "UNWRITTEN LAW" CONTINUES TO HOLD A POWERFUL SWAY.

THE THAW FAMILY'S LAWYERS, INEXPERIENCED IN THE CRIMINAL REALM, BRING IN AN OUTSIDE ATTORNEY...

LEWIS DELAFIELD, WHO PREPARES A DEFENSE OF INSANITY.

BUT HARRY ACCUSES HIM OF COLLUDING WITH THE STATE TO "RAILROAD" HIM INTO AN ASYLUM.

SO DELAFIELD IS FIRED, AND IN TIME A NEW MAN IS BROUGHT IN TO LEAD THE DEFENSE TEAM...

DELPHIN DELMAS OF SAN FRANCISCO, KNOWN AS "THE NAPOLEON OF THE WESTERN BAR," A SPECIALIST IN MURDER CASES. NO CLIENT OF HIS HAS EVER BEEN CONVICTED.

DELMAS THROWS OUT ANY REFERENCE TO INSANITY AND PLANS A DEFENSE BASED UPON AN INNOVATIVE INTERPRETATION OF THE "UNWRITTEN LAW."

IN IT, HARRY, UPON SPYING THE DEPRAVED ARCHITECT THAT NIGHT, WAS DRIVEN HELPLESSLY TO A "TEMPORARY BRAINSTORM."

THE DISTRICT ATTORNEY, WILLIAM T. JEROME, IS HAVING NONE OF THIS NONSENSE.

HE IS A YOUNG, AGGRESSIVE, INCORRUPTIBLE REFORMER IN THE MOLD OF PRESIDENT THEODORE ROOSEVELT.

(HE ALSO HAPPENS TO HAVE BEEN A CLOSE FRIEND OF STANFORD WHITE'S.)

HE PLANS TO PRESENT A STRAIGHTFORWARD PROSECUTION OF MURDER IN THE FIRST DEGREE.

AS THE TRIAL NEARS, EVELYN DUTIFULLY VISITS HER HUSBAND IN HIS CELL ALMOST EVERY DAY...

ENDURING THE SUFFOCATING CRUSH OF JOURNALISTS AND THE CURIOUS PUBLIC.

SPECULATION IS ACTIVE AS TO WHAT FINANCIAL AGREEMENT SHE HAS STRUCK WITH THE THAW FAMILY FOR HER CONTINUED SUPPORT OF HARRY'S DEFENSE.

SHE HAS REHEARSED HER TESTIMONY FOR COUNTLESS HOURS WITH ATTORNEY DELMAS.

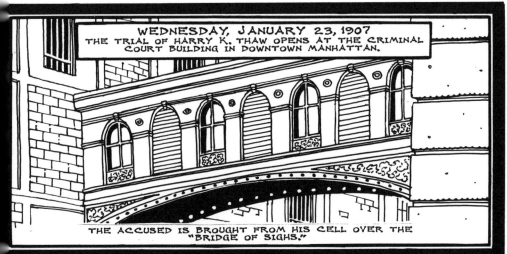

WEDNESDAY, JANUARY 23, 1907
THE TRIAL OF HARRY K. THAW OPENS AT THE CRIMINAL COURT BUILDING IN DOWNTOWN MANHATTAN.

THE ACCUSED IS BROUGHT FROM HIS CELL OVER THE "BRIDGE OF SIGHS."

JUSTICE JAMES FITZGERALD, OF THE NEW YORK SUPREME COURT, PRESIDES.

IN A DECISION THAT IS ALMOST UNPRECEDENTED, HE HAS ANNOUNCED THAT THE JURY WILL BE "INCARCERATED" (SEQUESTERED) FOR THE DURATION OF THE TRIAL.

CONSEQUENTLY, THE JURY-SELECTION PROCESS IS SLOW AND DIFFICULT.

AFTER EIGHT DAYS, A PANEL OF TWELVE GOOD MEN IS AT LAST SEATED...

A BROAD SELECTION OF SALESMEN, CLERKS, MANAGERS, AND AGENTS.

MONDAY, FEBRUARY 4
THE STATE DISPOSES OF ITS CASE BEFORE THE NOON RECESS.

FOUR WITNESSES FROM THE ROOF GARDEN DESCRIBE HAVING SEEN HARRY THAW SHOOT STANFORD WHITE.

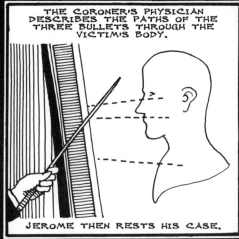

THE CORONER'S PHYSICIAN DESCRIBES THE PATHS OF THE THREE BULLETS THROUGH THE VICTIM'S BODY.

JEROME THEN RESTS HIS CASE.

IN THE AFTERNOON, THE OPENING STATEMENT FOR THE DEFENSE IS DELIVERED NOT BY THE FAMED ORATOR DELMAS BUT BY ONE OF THE THAW FAMILY LAWYERS, THE AGED JOHN GLEASON.

IT LEAVES MANY OBSERVERS PUZZLED.

WE WILL PROVE THAT HARRY THAW WAS INSANE WHEN HE KILLED STANFORD WHITE. WE WILL PROVE THAT HE WAS NOT ACCOUNTABLE FOR HIS ACTIONS, THAT HE BELIEVED HIMSELF TO BE AN AGENT OF PROVIDENCE.

A ROSTER OF DOCTORS AND ALIENISTS IS THEN CALLED...

WHO ATTEST TO THE DEFENDANT'S "NEUROTIC TEMPERAMENT."

OTHER WITNESSES DESCRIBE HARRY'S "IRRATIONAL" APPEARANCE ON THE NIGHT OF THE MURDER.

THURSDAY, FEBRUARY 7
THE DAY AWAITED BY EVERYONE ARRIVES, AS MRS. EVELYN NESBIT THAW TAKES THE STAND.

WATCHING IN THE COURTROOM ARE HER MOTHER AND BROTHER, NOW THOROUGHLY ESTRANGED FROM HER...

WHO HAVE COME IN SUPPORT OF THE GOOD NAME AND MEMORY OF STANFORD WHITE.

MR. DELMAS GUIDES THE WITNESS THROUGH HER EARLY FRIENDSHIP WITH HARRY THAW, HIS SEVERAL PROPOSALS...

AND FINALLY THE NIGHT IN PARIS WHEN SHE REVEALED TO HIM HER SEDUCTION AND VIOLATION BY WHITE.

SHE REPEATS THE SORDID TALE: HER FIRST MEETING WITH THE ARCHITECT...

THE NOTORIOUS RED VELVET SWING...

AND, FINALLY, THE TERRIBLE NIGHT IN THE MIRRORED BEDROOM.

SHE LEAVES THE IMPRESSION THAT HER ENTIRE RELATIONSHIP WITH THE OLDER MAN WAS AGAINST HER WILL.

WHAT WAS THE EFFECT OF THIS STATEMENT OF YOURS UPON MR. THAW?

HE BECAME VERY EXCITED.

WILL YOU KINDLY DESCRIBE IT?

HE WOULD GET UP AND WALK UP AND DOWN THE ROOM A MINUTE, AND THEN SIT DOWN AND SAY "OH GOD! OH GOD!" AND BITE HIS NAILS AND KEEP SOBBING.

THE COURTROOM LISTENS IN STUNNED SILENCE...

WHILE HARRY THAW WRITHES IN HIS CHAIR, AS IF HEARING IT ALL FOR THE FIRST TIME.

TUESDAY, FEBRUARY 19
AFTER MANY DELAYS, MR. JEROME
BEGINS THE CROSS-EXAMINATION.

BUT HE IS SEVERELY LIMITED IN ITS SCOPE DUE TO
MR. DELMAS'S INGENIOUS TACTIC ON DIRECT:

THE DEFENSE COUNSEL INSTRUCTED EVELYN TO
TESTIFY NOT AS TO THE TRUTH OF HER STORY...

BUT ONLY AS TO WHAT SHE HAD TOLD THE DEFENDANT.

THE DISTRICT ATTORNEY LEAPS FROM SUBJECT
TO SUBJECT, HIS QUESTIONS DESIGNED TO
HIGHLIGHT THE WITNESS'
ADVENTUROUS CAREER.

UP UNTIL THE TIME YOU WENT
INTO THE "FLORADORA" COMPANY
IN 1901, HAD YOU EVER POSED
IN THE NUDE?

NEVER!

DID YOU NOT HAVE A
PLASTER CAST MADE OF
YOURSELF IN THE NUDE
IN THE SPRING OF 1901?

I DID NOT!

EVELYN, LOOKING FRAIL AND DELICATE, MANAGES TO HOLD
HER OWN WITH DIGNITY AND SELF-POSSESSION.

ONCE, SHE COMES TO TEARS UNDER
A SERIES OF QUESTIONS ABOUT
STANFORD WHITE.

AFTER YOU HAD BEEN
WRONGED BY STANFORD
WHITE, DID YOU CONTINUE
TO HAVE INTIMATE
RELATIONS WITH HIM?

FOR A SHORT
TIME, YES.

DID YOU EVER TELL
ANY HUMAN BEING?

NO.

YOU ALWAYS
RESISTED AND NEVER
SUBMITTED WILLINGLY?

I ALWAYS
RESISTED.

AFTER FOUR FULL DAYS, SHE
IS DISMISSED FROM THE
STAND.

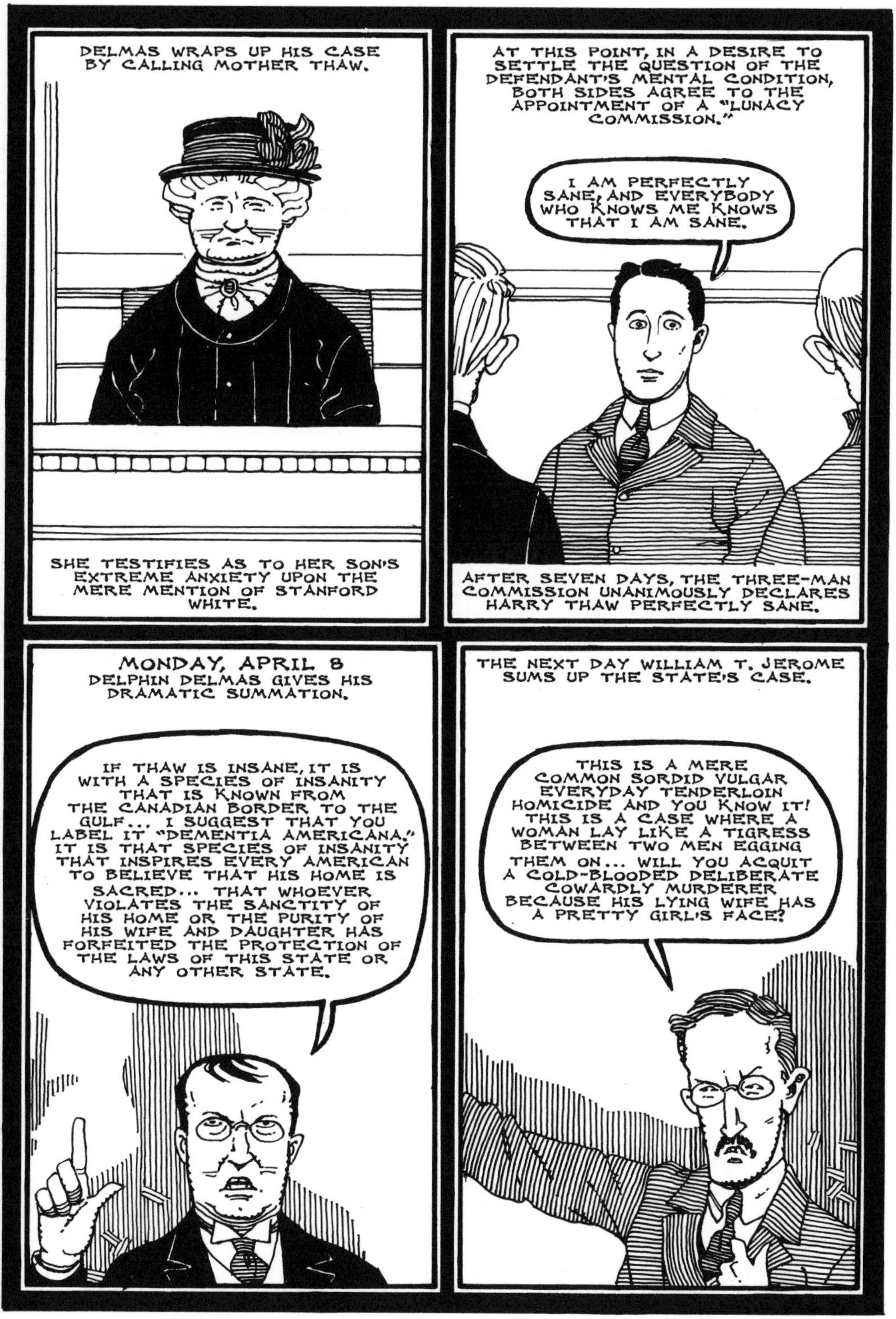
DELMAS WRAPS UP HIS CASE BY CALLING MOTHER THAW.
SHE TESTIFIES AS TO HER SON'S EXTREME ANXIETY UPON THE MERE MENTION OF STANFORD WHITE.
AT THIS POINT, IN A DESIRE TO SETTLE THE QUESTION OF THE DEFENDANT'S MENTAL CONDITION, BOTH SIDES AGREE TO THE APPOINTMENT OF A "LUNACY COMMISSION."
I AM PERFECTLY SANE, AND EVERYBODY WHO KNOWS ME KNOWS THAT I AM SANE.
AFTER SEVEN DAYS, THE THREE-MAN COMMISSION UNANIMOUSLY DECLARES HARRY THAW PERFECTLY SANE.
MONDAY, APRIL 8
DELPHIN DELMAS GIVES HIS DRAMATIC SUMMATION.
IF THAW IS INSANE, IT IS WITH A SPECIES OF INSANITY THAT IS KNOWN FROM THE CANADIAN BORDER TO THE GULF... I SUGGEST THAT YOU LABEL IT "DEMENTIA AMERICANA." IT IS THAT SPECIES OF INSANITY THAT INSPIRES EVERY AMERICAN TO BELIEVE THAT HIS HOME IS SACRED... THAT WHOEVER VIOLATES THE SANCTITY OF HIS HOME OR THE PURITY OF HIS WIFE AND DAUGHTER HAS FORFEITED THE PROTECTION OF THE LAWS OF THIS STATE OR ANY OTHER STATE.
THE NEXT DAY WILLIAM T. JEROME SUMS UP THE STATE'S CASE.
THIS IS A MERE COMMON SORDID VULGAR EVERYDAY TENDERLOIN HOMICIDE AND YOU KNOW IT! THIS IS A CASE WHERE A WOMAN LAY LIKE A TIGRESS BETWEEN TWO MEN EGGING THEM ON... WILL YOU ACQUIT A COLD-BLOODED DELIBERATE COWARDLY MURDERER BECAUSE HIS LYING WIFE HAS A PRETTY GIRL'S FACE?

WEDNESDAY, APRIL 10
AFTER JUSTICE FITZGERALD'S CHARGE, THE JURY RETIRES.

FRIDAY, APRIL 12
THEY RETURN TO TELL THE JUDGE THAT THEY ARE HOPELESSLY DEADLOCKED.

OF THE 12 MEN, SEVEN HAVE FOUND THAW GUILTY OF MURDER IN THE FIRST DEGREE, WHILE FIVE BELIEVE HIM NOT GUILTY BY REASON OF INSANITY.

IN A DAZE, EVELYN KISSES HER HUSBAND.

HARRY, ANGRY AND FRUSTRATED, IS DENIED BAIL AND RETURNED TO HIS CELL.

DELMAS WILL SOON BE OUT AS HEAD OF THE DEFENSE.

OVER THE NINE MONTHS DURING WHICH THE DEFENDANT AWAITS A SECOND TRIAL, HIS WIFE VISITS HIM REGULARLY.

STILL SUPPORTED BY THE THAW FAMILY, SHE KNOWS THAT SHE WILL BE CALLED UPON ONCE AGAIN TO PLAY THE ROLE OF LOYAL SPOUSE.

MONDAY, JANUARY 6, 1908. THE SECOND TRIAL OF HARRY THAW OPENS.

IT WILL PROVE TO BE A FASTER, MORE COMPACT VERSION OF THE FIRST ONE.

PRESIDING THIS TIME: JUSTICE VICTOR J. DOWLING OF THE NEW YORK SUPREME COURT.

THE NEW LEADER OF THE DEFENSE TEAM IS MARTIN W. LITTLETON...

ASSISTED BY RUSSELL PEABODY AND DANIEL O'REILLY.

WILLIAM JEROME, EAGER FOR A SECOND CHANCE, AGAIN TAKES UP THE PROSECUTION.

A JURY IS CHOSEN IN A MERE FOUR DAYS.

THE DISTRICT ATTORNEY ONCE MORE PRESENTS A STRAIGHTFORWARD CASE OF MURDER IN THE FIRST DEGREE.

WHILE THE DEFENSE, HAVING ABANDONED THE "UNWRITTEN LAW," INTRODUCES MEMBERS OF THE THAW FAMILY...

WHO AFFIRM THE STRAINS ON INSANITY IN THEIR LINEAGE.

EVELYN IS, ONCE AGAIN, THE CENTER OF ATTENTION. BY ALL ACCOUNTS, SHE SEEMS MORE RELAXED AND SELF-ASSURED THAN FOR THE FIRST TRIAL.

HER TESTIMONY IS A REPETITION OF HER PREVIOUS ACCOUNT, SOME SAY WORD-FOR-WORD.

MR. JEROME CROSS-EXAMINES WITH ALL OF HIS FORMER ANTAGONISM.

AND YOU HAD GONE AWAY FROM LONDON WITH THAW AS HIS MISTRESS?!

YES.

AS HIS MISTRESS?!

MORE THAN ONCE HE CRACKS HER COMPOSURE.

MR. JEROME, I DON'T UNDERSTAND YOU. I TRY TO, BUT I CAN'T UNDERSTAND YOU. I REFUSE TO ANSWER YOUR QUESTION UNTIL I CAN FIND OUT WHAT YOU MEAN.

FRIDAY, JANUARY 31
THE CASE GOES TO THE JURY.

SATURDAY, FEBRUARY 1
THE VERDICT IS DELIVERED.

WE THE JURY FIND THE DEFENDANT NOT GUILTY AS CHARGED IN THE INDICTMENT, ON THE GROUND OF THE DEFENDANT'S INSANITY.

JUSTICE DOWLING PRONOUNCES THE SENTENCE: HARRY THAW WILL BE TRANSPORTED FORTHWITH TO THE MATTEAWAN ASYLUM FOR THE CRIMINALLY INSANE...

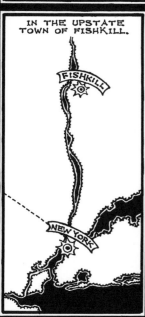

IN THE UPSTATE TOWN OF FISHKILL.

FISHKILL

NEW YORK

HARRY MAKES THE TRIP IN A PRIVATE RAILROAD CAR FILLED WITH FRIENDS AND JOURNALISTS.

I'LL BE OUT IN A FEW WEEKS.

HARRY IS AFFORDED HIS OWN ROOM AT MATTEAWAN, FURNISHED TO HIS COMFORT.

EVELYN TAKES A ROOM IN FISHKILL, THE BETTER TO VISIT HER HUSBAND REGULARLY...

WHILE A NEW SET OF LAWYERS BEGINS A LONG SERIES OF APPEALS AND WRITS OF HABEAS CORPUS.

ALL OF WHICH WILL BE DENIED.

IT IS A SLOW AND LABORIOUS PROCESS, BECAUSE VERY FEW OF THE PEOPLE INVOLVED, EVEN HIS MOTHER AND HIS WIFE...

WANT TO SEE HARRY SET LOOSE.

AS THE MONTHS DRAG ON, STRAINS UPON THE MARRIAGE BECOME EVIDENT.

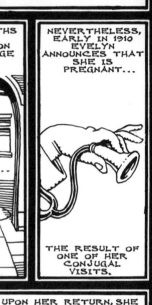
NEVERTHELESS, EARLY IN 1910 EVELYN ANNOUNCES THAT SHE IS PREGNANT...

THE RESULT OF ONE OF HER CONJUGAL VISITS.

HARRY VEHEMENTLY DENIES THAT HE IS THE FATHER...

AND, FURTHER, ACCUSES HIS WIFE OF TRYING TO EXTORT MONEY FROM THE THAW FAMILY.

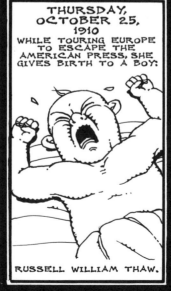
THURSDAY, OCTOBER 25, 1910
WHILE TOURING EUROPE TO ESCAPE THE AMERICAN PRESS, SHE GIVES BIRTH TO A BOY.

RUSSELL WILLIAM THAW.

UPON HER RETURN, SHE AND HER SON RESIDE IN NEW YORK, WHILE SHE TRIES TO REVIVE HER THEATRICAL CAREER.

STAGE DOOR

SUNDAY, AUGUST 17, 1913
IMPATIENT WITH THE LEGAL MACHINERY, HARRY THAW ESCAPES FROM MATTEAWAN.

AS A DUMFOUNDED GUARD WATCHES, THE PRISONER SIMPLY STROLLS THROUGH THE FRONT GATE...

AND INTO A WAITING AUTOMOBILE.

HE IS DRIVEN ACROSS THE INTERNATIONAL BORDER, TO THE TOWN OF SHERBROOKE IN QUEBEC....

WHERE HE IS FETED AS A CELEBRITY.

NEVERTHELESS, HE MUST WAIT IN A CELL WHILE AN EXTRADITION HEARING DETERMINES HIS FATE.

DISTRICT ATTORNEY JEROME IS ONCE AGAIN PRESENT FOR THE PROSECUTION.

EVENTUALLY, THAW IS DEPORTED FROM CANADA TO NEW HAMPSHIRE...

AND, FINALLY, IN DECEMBER OF 1914, TO NEW YORK FOR YET A THIRD TRIAL...

THIS ONE FOR HIS VERY SANITY.

FRIDAY, JULY 16, 1915

AFTER A PROCEEDING THAT IS MORE OR LESS A COPY OF THE FIRST TWO, HARRY THAW, AGE 44, IS DECLARED SANE AND ACQUITTED OF ALL CHARGES.

IN PITTSBURGH, A CHEERING CROWD WELCOMES HIM HOME.

HE AND EVELYN ARE AT LAST DIVORCED.

HAVING RECEIVED BUT A PITTANCE IN SETTLEMENT FROM THE THAW FAMILY, EVELYN, AT AGE 36, IS PLUNGED ONCE AGAIN AGAIN INTO A HAND-TO-MOUTH EXISTENCE...

THIS TIME AS A SINGLE MOTHER.

FOR SEVERAL YEARS, SHE MANAGES TO LIVE UPON HER NOTORIETY.

THE STORY OF MY LIFE

EVELYN THAW

SHE RELEASES A MEMOIR IN 1914.

SHE APPEARS IN A NUMBER OF MOVING PICTURES, AS VERSIONS OF HERSELF.

SHE TOURS THE COUNTRY AS PART OF A VAUDEVILLE DANCING ACT.

HER PARTNER, JACK CLIFFORD, BECOMES HER SECOND HUSBAND IN 1916.

BUT THE UNION IS A TROUBLED ONE, AND THEY SEPARATE IN 1918...

FINALLY DIVORCING IN 1933.

FOR THE REMAINDER OF HIS LIFE, HARRY THAW CANNOT MANAGE TO STAY OUT OF THE HEADLINES.

IN 1917, HE IS INDICTED FOR THE KIDNAPPING AND WHIPPING OF A 19-YEAR-OLD YOUTH, FREDERICK GUMP, AT A NEW YORK HOTEL.

AS A RESULT, HE IS COMMITTED TO THE MENTAL WARD OF THE PENNSYLVANIA STATE HOSPITAL IN PHILADELPHIA, FOR WHAT TURNS OUT TO BE SEVEN YEARS.

IN 1926, HE PRODUCES A DISJOINTED MEMOIR, IN WHICH HE DECLARES HIMSELF A BENEFACTOR OF THE HUMAN RACE.

THE TRAITOR

HARRY K. THAW

(THE TITLE REFERS TO HIS FIRST TRIAL LAWYER, DELAFIELD, WHO TRIED TO PAINT HIM AS INSANE.)

IN 1929, HE IS SUED BY A WOMAN, MARCIA ESTARDUS, WHO CLAIMS THAT HE BEAT HER IN HER NEW YORK APARTMENT.

AFTER THREE TRIALS, A SETTLEMENT IS PAID TO THE PLAINTIFF.

IN 1937, HE IS SUED BY A HOTEL HEADWAITER, FOR INJURIES SUSTAINED FROM A FURIOUS PHYSICAL ASSAULT BY THE MILLIONAIRE.

HARRY THAW DIES AT AGE 76, ON FEBRUARY 22, 1947, SUFFERING A HEART ATTACK WHILE ON A VISIT TO MIAMI, FLORIDA.

78

WHILE TRYING TO SCRAPE TOGETHER A LIVING, SHE ENDURES PERIODS OF ALCOHOL AND MORPHINE ABUSE.

IN 1934, SHE BRINGS OUT A SECOND MEMOIR.

ON THE STRENGTH OF HER NAME, SHE MANAGES A SERIES OF NIGHTCLUBS AND SPEAKEASIES.

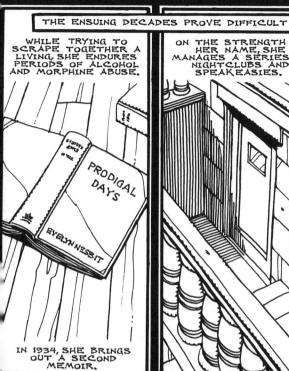

SHE TOURS IN A CABARET ACT SINGING NUMBERS LIKE:

"I'M JUST A BROAD-MINDED BROAD FROM BROADWAY..."

IN 1955, SHE SERVES AS TECHNICAL ADVISOR FOR THE MOTION PICTURE "THE GIRL IN THE RED VELVET SWING," BASED IN PART UPON HER MEMOIRS.

SHE IS PORTRAYED BY THE RISING STARLET JOAN COLLINS.

EVELYN'S LAST YEARS ARE SPENT IN LOS ANGELES...

WHERE SHE PURSUES A LONG-HIDDEN TALENT AS PAINTER, SCULPTOR, AND CERAMIC ARTIST.

SHE DIES ON JANUARY 17, 1967, AT THE AGE OF 82.

79

MONUMENTS TO THE THREE PLAYERS IN THIS DRAMA CAN BE VISITED TODAY.

STANFORD WHITE'S STANDS IN THE GRAVEYARD OF THE ST. JAMES EPISCOPAL CHURCH, SUFFOLK COUNTY, LONG ISLAND.

THAT OF HENRY (HARRY) KENDALL THAW IS PART OF HIS FAMILY'S PLOT AT ALLEGHENY CEMETERY IN PITTSBURGH, PENNSYLVANIA.

HENRY KENDALL THAW

FEBRUARY 12 - 1871

FEBRUARY 22 - 1947

AND NOW ABIDETH FAITH, HOPE CHARITY, THESE THREE, BUT THE GREATEST OF THESE IS CHARITY.

MOTHER
EVELYN FLORENCE NESBIT
1884 † 1967

THE MARKER FOR EVELYN FLORENCE NESBIT CAN BE FOUND AT THE HOLY CROSS CEMETERY IN CULVER CITY, CALIFORNIA.